Blessings for a

Mother's Day

~

Ruth Bell Graham

WORD PUBLISHING

NASHVILLE

A Thomas Nelson Company

Introduction

~

Although the joys far outweigh the cares, and parenting (and grandparenting) continues to be my most rewarding occupation, I do not always find it easy. Parenthood is a big responsibility. It is demanding physically, emotionally, and spiritually. At times, it is overwhelming. But God, who is ever true to His Word and so faithful, has always provided the needed strength and wisdom to see me through each trial. God also provided an excellent role model, my mother, Ruth Bell Graham.

Sometimes, when I experience a rather difficult day and wonder if it is all worth it, I allow my mind to drift back to the mountains of North Carolina, to our old log cabin where I grew up. My mother created a special refuge for her husband and children. Our home provided for our physical, emotional, and material needs;

but more than that, it provided for our spiritual needs. The framework of our home was our godly Christian heritage.

My mother has been faithful in passing on to her daughters all that she learned and gleaned from her mother (Virginia Bell) and from the various saints she has read down through the years. Mother shares by example as well as through her words. She was once asked how she had raised five children with my daddy away so much of the time. Without hesitation she answered, "On my knees."

My son Aram once described home as "a place where you come in out of the rain." The home in which I was raised was a warm sanctuary from the storms of life for each member of our family. In the following pages, you can glimpse how one small, feisty, humorous, intelligent, deeply spiritual pilgrim of faith approached the task of mothering and how she became (and continues to be to this day) my role model and best friend.

—*Gigi Graham Tchividjian*

My Mother Was a Remarkable Woman

❧

Born in Richmond, Virginia, raised first in Charlottesville, then in Waynesboro, she and Daddy got engaged when they were sixteen and eighteen. While he went through The Medical College of Virginia in Richmond, she went to the Assembly Training School there and took a year of nursing. She and Daddy were married in 1916 and that fall sailed to China on the *Mauritania*. Daddy was twenty-two.

Mother was a slim 114 pounds. "Poor little Virginia Bell!" one missionary is reported to have exclaimed. "She won't last a year!"

She fooled them. She not only lasted a year, she lasted twenty-five of them before returning to the States to live another thirty-three years. I do not believe in drafting women into the army. But God sure has them in His. And Mother was one of them. She was strong-minded, had definite opinions of her own, and was outspoken and hard-working.

Furthermore, she was married to Daddy, who was strong-minded, had definite opinions of his own, and was outspoken and hard-working.

Mother was the self-appointed censor of all books that arrived at our mission station in China. If they passed her, she passed them along. If they failed her, she burned them. That is how the missionaries missed *Gone with the Wind*. That is how I missed it, and I've never gotten around to reading it yet.

Mother ran the home, no easy task when one considers we had no running water. Every piece of laundry washed in the hospital had to be carefully inspected for bedbugs on return. Fresh groceries had to be purchased daily from the local market by Yang Er, the cook. (He caught sight of a foreign face and presto—inflation!) Therefore money for food had to be apportioned daily and accounted for when the cook returned from market. Water hauled from the Grand Canal had to be carried in two buckets suspended from the ends of bamboo poles (called *bien-dans*) balanced on the shoulders of the water carriers, deposited in two large earthenware jars, sprinkled with alum to make the mud settle, then boiled at least twenty minutes and filtered through cotton two or three times before it was drinkable. Since the canal was not only a waterway for boats but a sewage system, a garbage dump, and even a cemetery for small unwanted bodies, such precaution was understandable. All fruits, raw vegetables, and berries had to be carefully washed in this purified canal water.

Further, Yang Er had to be taught to cook Western dishes. Though we enjoyed Chinese food (I think we children preferred it), the usual menu was comparable to what we would eat in America. The southern part of America, that is.

Water was heated in the tank on the side of the old Majestic iron kitchen range. For one's daily ablutions as well as the weekly bath, water had to be transferred into tin containers and carried upstairs. We children shared the same bath water. To do otherwise would have been extravagant. I can't remember whether we went from oldest to youngest or from cleanest to dirtiest. I do remember how, in the winter when the old tin tubs were placed beside the little tin trash burner in one's bedroom, one tended to freeze on one side and blister on the other. And the trash burner was exactly what the name implied. When one ran out of burnable trash, small bundles of dried soybean stocks were a fine substitute.

All canned goods (even our butter and milk came in cans) had to be ordered in quantity from Shanghai. Being raised on Carnation milk, it took me some time to become accustomed to fresh milk, which by comparison is tasteless.

We always had someone else living with us. Another missionary couple or a single missionary. Or both.

Mother taught us through the sixth grade. She was a rough teacher. Along with schoolwork, she taught us to crochet, knit, embroider, and sew. That was in the mornings.

In the afternoons she donned her Chinese cotton dress and headed for the Women's Clinic, which she supervised. I still have the white linen Chinese dress she wore in the summertime. Daddy always said Mother was the best diagnostician he knew. Most of the cases were simple lancing of boils, prescribing for worms, treating of trachoma, etc.

On returning to the house, without fail, she changed, bathed, and put on fresh clothes.

Mother ran a tight ship. We arose on time and had breakfast together on time, followed by family prayers, which, during the week, included a hymn. (Mother played the piano and had a fine soprano voice while Daddy was an excellent baritone, so singing was a part of the family life.) After the singing of a hymn, Daddy read a portion of Scripture, followed by prayer.

On Sundays this was lengthened to each person selecting a hymn, a chapter and verse to be read by each member of the family in turn, and longer prayers. Our Chinese helpers joined us on these occasions, though how much they got out of it is questionable.

One afternoon a week there was stationed a prayer meeting that met alternately in the various missionary homes. Otherwise Mother used this time to write letters back to the States, or, after we had left for school, to write to us. And as far back as I can remember she kept a diary. Everyone dressed for dinner in the evening. It was the big meal of the day. And after dinner it was family time. Daddy had his hospital rounds to make, but on returning we would sit around the open fire in the wintertime. We "womenfolk" did handwork (knitting, embroidery, braiding rugs, crocheting, sewing) while the men took turns reading aloud (Scott, Dickens, Uncle Remus, *Ben Hur*, etc.).

Mother had five children at home. She would not hear of

going to a hospital, nor would she hear of having anyone but Daddy delivering the babies.

The third one, Nelson Junior, died at ten months and is buried in Tsingkiang.

All this and not one day during her twenty-five years in China did she know what it was not to have a splitting headache.

Love the LORD your God with all your heart and with all your soul and with all your strength. These commandments that I give you today are to be upon your hearts. Impress them on your children. Talk about them when you sit at home and when you walk along the road, when you lie down and when you get up.

—DEUTERONOMY 6:5–7

Help Me Be a Good Girl

❧

I wish Jesus would come into this world and you would take me to see Him," declared Gigi. "I would make Him stoop down and I would whisper in His ear."

"And what would you whisper?" I asked.

"I would say, 'Dear Jesus, would You please help me be a good girl?'"

Why is it harder for some to be good than others?

The Old Parks Cottage

~

We finally bought the old Parks cottage, just across Louisiana Road from Lao E and Lao Niang on a big corner lot with tall oak trees and a stream protected on two sides from the road by a big wall of rhododendron bushes.

We added two bedrooms and a small bath on the front; tore down partitions in the old section to make a generous V-shaped living room with a raised, hooded, stone fireplace in the center; and had a small room left for a utility room, kitchen, and dining room. That made up the downstairs. Upstairs we redecorated but left it pretty much as it was until we had paid off the bank.

Working enthusiastically, I was ready for us to move in when I came back from the hospital with Anne. Gigi's bassinet, freshly trimmed with some of my bridal veil over quilted blue satin and freshly made up with my first attempt at hand-monogrammed sheets and pillowcase, was standing to the left of the wide picture window in Bill's and my bedroom. The walls were Wedgwood blue. Lao Niang had given me the old Victorian bedroom suite from her house. This we had painted white. We had made the draw curtains and the dust ruffles ourselves. (The dust ruffles hid the fact that the box springs rested on cinder blocks.) The bedside tables were made out of an old-fashioned dresser, the kind that has a set of drawers on either side and an almost full-length mirror between. The mirror was removed and the dresser cut in two, painted white except for the top, which matched the Wedgwood blue walls. The bedside lamps were made out of old cardboard cylinders in which Lao E got adhesive for his doctor's office in Asheville. These I had wired with supplies from the dime store, wound with laundry rope, painted Wedgwood blue, then twisted a single strand of roses from the dime store around them, touching them up with nail polish and clear shellac to give the impression of ceramic flowers. They were topped by white dime-store shades trimmed with organdy ruffles.

In fact I made nearly every lamp in the house (except for the permanent fixtures). An old iron sugar bowl was one, with two matching plates to hang on the wall behind it; old bottles (the easiest), earthen jugs (also easy), and outside lighting fixtures made out of tin cans cut with tin shears and twisted into shapes, painted with flat black paint made to appear like wrought-iron fixtures. Bill used to say he could always tell the light fixtures I made, as they were the ones that went out when you turned them on.

That was a detour.

Anyway, once comfortably in the privacy of our own bedroom at home with Anne, either beside me or in the bassinet, and Bill and Gigi looking after us both, it was a bit of heaven!

Bill, a little more accustomed to babies by now, held Anne less gingerly, more comfortably. And Gigi, just tall enough to peer over the bassinet, kept checking to make sure Anne was still there.

Empathy

~

Supper was over and the small, round dining-room table cleared. As we washed the dishes and straightened the kitchen, suddenly Gigi, age six, slugged Anne.

So I sentenced her to sit in her chair for five minutes. Forced inactivity for a child who woke up running and went to sleep running was sheer torture.

Without Gigi, her adored playmate, Anne was lost. In a few minutes she slipped up to me, confiding in her soft voice, "Muffa, I said 'stinky.' Can I sit in the chair, too?" Permission granted, she ran happily over to Gigi.

"It's all right, Gigi," she announced in her gentle way. "I will sit with you."

How's that for empathy?

Grant your strength to your servant.

—PSALM 86:16

Punishment

~

There was the time Gigi and I took the bus from Charlotte back to Black Mountain. It was November 6, 1951. She was six. We boarded the bus in Charlotte and headed for home. She was unendurable, to put it mildly. Nothing suited her, and she made no effort pretending it did.

A few friendly passengers remarked to me that I surely had my hands full. "One more passenger comments on your behavior," I hissed at her, "and you've had it!"

Instant transformation.

But no sooner had we reached the mountain and settled in the little gray house in the valley when she started scrapping with Anne. I knew there lacked only one more straw to break this camel's back. It wasn't long in coming. She sassed me (an item I considered in the "morals" bracket) and, furthermore, flatly contradicted me. That did it. She got snapped out of her mood as sweet as pie.

That night as we prayed before supper, I asked God to help us be sweet.

Anne looked up.

"Mother," she said in her own gentle, inimitable way, "you aren't a sweet girl. You spank people."

"She has to, Anne!" Gigi interjected authoritatively. "God told her to. If she doesn't punish us when we are bad, God will punish her."

Bunny

~

$\mathcal{B}$ill called long-distance to say he was sending us a Great Pyrenees. ("The most gorgeous dog I have ever seen," he exclaimed.)

Beatrice Long had come to help us out, and I realized another little Graham was on the way, all in that one week.

I wanted a dog like I wanted a chimpanzee or water buffalo. But the day he was to arrive by freight, the two girls, Beatrice, and I piled into the car and headed for the Asheville Freight Depot.

"We are looking for a little white puppy from New England," I said.

"We got no little white puppy," the freight master replied. We didn't know whether to be elated or disappointed when an overalled character leaning against the depot looked us over, spit, and drawled, "There's a big white dog 'round yonder in a box."

Our "little white puppy" turned out to be the "big white dog." Three months of overgrown feet, long white hair, soulful eyes, sloppy tongue, and a bare tail.

"Looks like a carrot," Bea observed of the tail.

"Sure does," I agreed. "An inverted one."

There was a lot of adjusting to be done all around: Bea adjusting to us; us adjusting to the new dog (which we decided to name Belshazzar, as it suited him); me, a little seasick at the time, adjusting to the whole situation; and Belshazzar in turn adjusting to us.

Beatrice turned out to be an institution. She remained with us through thick and thin throughout the next thirty years. I didn't train her; she trained me. She never hurried, but she always got things done. She never raised her voice, but she had the children's love and respect and therefore, usually, their obedience.

When Bunny arrived December 19, I think Beatrice was as proud as I. When I first saw Gigi, she had filled me with awe; with Anne, I had felt perfectly relaxed; but Bunny had us all chuckling.

She was tiny and red-faced with masses of black hair. Even down to her little pink earlobes was this soft dark down. But her wistful little expression made us think of a baby rabbit, so "Bunny" she was from that day on.

"My! What an ugly baby!" exclaimed Mother.

"She looks just exactly like you, Mother," I replied.

"You know," admitted Mother, "I can see it myself."

It was nearing Christmas. Because of the circumstances, I had "attended to my little errands of love" early that year. Mother was having us for Christmas dinner. We were home from the hospital in two days (special dispensation), and Bunny and I lay on the sofa beneath the picture window in front of the open fire, the tree just behind us, listening to Christmas carols playing softly by the hour. Everyone should have one Christmas baby. You feel very close to Mary.

Prayer with Franklin

~

A very small Franklin had great difficulty being still through any prayer. It is a real job teaching reverence to so much exuberance.

Then one night he suggested I pray. All through the prayer he made little *arp! arp!* noises like a baby seal. With each *arp* I would stop. In what I hoped was menacing, disapproving silence, he was quite still. Then as soon as I resumed, *arp!*

As soon as I finished, over the bed he went and under, apparently looking for something that had just disappeared and eagerly in search of it.

"I heard something go *'arp! arp!'*" he exclaimed.

Grapefruit

~

All the children wanted grapefruit one morning, and there was only one.

"That's all right," Franklin said matter-of-factly. "I'll have it."

The spirit of gracious and expressed affection, let no one shrink from expressing it! The heart has strange abysses of gloom and often yearns for just one word of love to help. And it is just when the manner may be drier and less genial than usual that the need may be the greatest.

—Lucy C. Smith

A Hectic Morning

〜

It had been one of those hectic nights, and I had over-slept. Without fixing my hair or pausing for makeup, I hurriedly pulled on my bathrobe, lifted Franklin out of his bed without bothering to change him, and set him in the high chair. I proceeded to set the table hurriedly for breakfast so the children would not be late for school.

That morning, every time Gigi opened her mouth to say something, Bunny interrupted. Finally, in exasperation, Gigi slammed down her fork.

"Mother!" she exclaimed. "Between listening to Bunny and smelling Franklin and looking at you, I'm not hungry!"

And Then There Were Five

~~~

*P*eople ask me if I did not suffer terribly from loneliness when Bill was away. Occasionally I went to bed with his tweed jacket for company.

But there was little opportunity for loneliness with little Grahams underfoot. And with five little Grahams went an assortment of animal friends and an assortment of people friends as well.

I treasure those years. There were the times of unbelievable bliss when a little snugly wrapped bundle would be laid in my arms, and I would lie there studying each tiny pink finger, each damp eyelash, watching the heartbeat in the top of the little head through the soft fuzz of hair.

And with each one I knew instinctively his or her general character: Gigi would be smarter and wiser than I was; Anne was gentle and loving; Bunny (my namesake who got her nickname because she looked like a rabbit when she was born) brought a special touch of joy. Franklin was the first son, and a strapping one at that, and I knew he would be a handful but would grow to be someone who could be depended upon.

Five years later Ned arrived, a sort of happy P.S., and I knew that God had given us a final and very special blessing.

The children taught me much as they were growing up: about themselves, about the world around them, about me, and especially about God.

Do not be afraid. Stand firm and you will see the deliverance the LORD will bring you today. . . .
The LORD will fight for you; you need only to be still.

—EXODUS 14:13, 14

Self-Indulgence and Self-Control

~

*D*ear Journal,

Reading again from Exodus 33:12–16. This job of training five little Grahams to be good soldiers of Jesus Christ is too big for me, when I am not a good soldier myself. Feeling particularly distracted (or I should say overwhelmed and confused) this morning, I have been looking to the Lord asking, "Where, from here?"

Bill will be leaving soon for the San Francisco meeting. And I almost have a sinking feeling. Not altogether a left-behind and left-out sort of feeling, but swamped, knowing that all the things I have depended on others to do, I shall have to do myself.

And things have not been going smoothly. There is a terrible amount of fighting among the children, ugliness and back talk from Gigi, and peevishness on my part backed by sporadic, uncertain discipline. (Mr. Sawyer said in speaking of his mother the other day, "When she said 'whoa' we knew she meant 'whoa.'")

I am not walking the Lord's way at all. I am doing what I feel like doing rather than what I ought to do. These verses hit me hard: "She who is self-indulgent is dead even while she lives" (1 Tim. 5:6 RSV), and "The fruit of the Spirit is . . . self-control" (Gal. 5:22, 23).

Self-indulgence is doing what we want rather than what we ought. I had always thought of self-control applying to temper or to drink. But what about the almonds in the pantry, the ice cream and chocolate sauce, the candy that I know will add unnecessary pounds and make my face break out? What about controlling my tongue? My tone of voice? Standing up straight? Writing letters? All these and many more need controlling.

And I don't look well to the ways of my household. Children well-taught even to brushing teeth and keeping rooms straight. Regular family prayers at the supper table. Children's clothes kept mended and neat and organized. Getting ready for Sunday on Saturday. Well, there's no use going into it all. It just boils down to the fact that I am not being a good mother.

So I took it to Him this morning. I want above everything to be the kind of person He wants. If He had His undisputed way in me, I would be. Everything would solve itself. The place to begin is here; the time to begin is now. And as I reread Exodus 33:12–16, the phrase that jumped out at me, which I had never noticed before, was: "Shew me now thy way" (v. 13, KJV).

P.S. I could not help but chuckle when I read a quote from

Mr. Abba Eban in the *London Times* (June 13, 1980): "Israelis are not renowned for any spontaneous tendency to agree with one another." Neither are little Grahams.

TV Guides

~

Dear Journal,
It was around bedtime when I heard Franklin crying. Gigi had choked him for giving Anne his *TV Guide*. She claimed he had promised all of his to her.

My first reaction was to go upstairs and thrash her, deprive her of Monday's TV privileges, and no telling what else. I was angry. Angry at ugliness after so much beauty and blessing over the weekend. Angry with her, the oldest, for being so mean and selfish.

So I continued nursing Ned and prayed hard for guidance. "Lord, show me now Thy way." Then I called them all downstairs.

These *TV Guides*, apart from their initial usefulness, have been nothing but a source of contention. They read them, study the pictures, collect favorites to be their husbands, brothers, etc., etc. So I laid down the law. All were to be burned.

It was Gigi, of course, who went dramatic on me. She flatly refused. Said I was stealing. Wished she were back in Hampden DuBose School. Christian homes were no fun. And so on and on.

So we got on our knees, and each asked the Lord what He would have us do with the old guides and piles of treasured pictures. Anne and Bunny "came up" deciding to burn them. Gigi, however, still insisted Jesus doesn't take away all our fun and that He wouldn't mind their keeping the better pictures.

But this is all surface. It's her spiritual development about which I am primarily concerned. How to encourage her Bible study and prayer life. How to help her choose His way. And my ability is definitely limited. I may be able to make her make up her bed and keep her from bad movies. But I cannot make her be unselfish, loving, and considerate. I can—up to a point—take care of the outside. But I am wholly dependent upon the Lord to work in her heart "to will and to do His good pleasure."

If only God will enable me to tend to the possible, depending on Him for the impossible.

Pacifist or Peacemaker?

～～

Dear Journal,

Ruth Peale, at the Layman's Institute of Miami (January 13–16, 1960), stated in her most helpful and refreshing address that "the home should be a place of quiet peacefulness."

And so it should. Ours is an island all right—but at times more like Alcatraz, I think.

Furthermore, the Bible backs up Ruth Peale's statement.

"Better is a dry morsel, and quietness therewith, than an house full of sacrifices ["feasting" RSV] with strife" (Prov. 17:1 KJV), and "He that troubleth his own house shall inherit the wind" (Prov. 11:29 KJV). Knox translation has it: "He shall feed

on air, that misrules his own household," while Lamsa's Aramaic translation puts it, "He who fails to make his household tranquil shall bequeath the wind to his children."

This responsibility falls squarely on the mother's shoulders. Uncomfortably, whenever Proverbs speaks of nagging ("It is better to dwell in a corner of the housetop, than in a house shared with a contentious woman"), it is the woman to whom Solomon is referring. There is no getting around it. The woman creates the atmosphere in the home.

Unfortunately, I seem to have been infected with a kind of deadly spiritual pacifism, an unwillingness to roll up my sleeves and lick the socks off the devil—or die trying. Here is our home. The thing is almost out of hand scrapping among the children. It may be natural. It is also sinful.

There is a vital difference between "pacifist" and "peacemaker." Occasionally the peacemaker has to whip the daylights out of the troublemakers in order to have peace. And Jesus never said, "Blessed are the pacifists" but "Blessed are the peacemakers."

Isaiah 41:15 has helped put a bit of "fight" in me: With God's help, we can "thresh the mountains, and beat them small" (KJV).

Psalm 18:43: "Thou hast delivered me from the strivings of the people." Verse 47: "It is God that . . . subdueth the people under me" (KJV).

We can lick this evil. With His help we will. A happy, well-disciplined, well-ordered, loving home is our spiritual right.

In Deuteronomy 3:28,
God says to Moses,
"Charge Joshua . . . encourage him . . .
strengthen him."
So must parents their children.

Wanting to Learn

~

One day Anne lunched with friends and me at a local hotel, disgruntled because Bunny couldn't go with us. She was rude, boorish, and disagreeable (all in a sweet sort of way). As we got in the car, she said, "Mother, I behaved really dreadfully today, didn't I?"

Her conscience still on the job, she came to me at bedtime. "Mother," she begged, "now please tell me everything I did wrong. I want to know. I want to learn."

How often do I come to God at the close of day in that spirit?

Dog Training

~

$\mathcal{D}$ear Journal,

Every parent should read at least one good book on dog training. Odd how, in a day when children are notoriously disobedient, dog training and obedience classes are increasing in popularity. Basically the rules are simple:

1. Keep commands simple and at a minimum. One word to a command and always the same word. Come. Sit. Stay. Heel. Down. No. (I talk my children dizzy.)

2. Be consistent.

3. Be persistent. Follow through. Never give a command without seeing it is obeyed.

4. When the dog responds correctly, praise him. (Not with food. Remember, don't reward children materially for doing well. Your praise should be enough.)

It is a fine kettle of fish when our dogs are better trained than our children.

Hard to Be Good

~

I had been extra hard on Anne one day when she was small. The details have evaporated with the years. All, that is, except a small girl's tearful comment as I tucked her in bed: "Mother, you make it so hard to be good!"

Someone has said, "A Christian is one who makes it easy to believe in Jesus."

Perhaps it could also be said, "A good mother is one who makes it easy for a child to be good."

I would get so tired taking care of the children, the house, the wear and tear of mothering and homemaking—in fact, one doctor said it is normal for young mothers to be tired. This verse was a great comfort to me: "Now therefore, O our God, the great, mighty and awesome God. . . . Do not let all this hardship seem trifling in your eyes" (Neh. 9:32).

Bye, Daddy!

~

"Bye, Daddy!"

Bill was home more than most people realize, but not as much as we would have liked.

I vividly recall our small, blonde-haired girl sitting in the grass, her translucent blue eyes fixed on a plane overhead and far away. In a wistful little voice she was calling, "Bye, Daddy! Bye, Daddy!"

A plane implied that Daddy was on it, going somewhere. How much we missed him, only each one knows.

Born Good

~

Bunny was born good. I should write one chapter called "Don't Take Advantage of the Good Child." But perhaps sometimes mothers need to. Perhaps that's why God sends a particularly good one here and there along the line.

Bunny played in her crib by the hour as a baby, never asking for anything. She was the sort of child who kept her room neat without being told, obeyed promptly, and had a marvelous disposition coupled with a ridiculous sense of humor.

Mr. Rickman, who took care of us for many years, cutting the lawn, scraping the snow off the roads in the winter, driving the kids to school in the jeep, and even helping with the heavy housework, taught each of the children to drive at an early age.

At that time, one of the association's secretaries lived with us. A friend was visiting her. I had to go down to Jackson, Mississippi, to speak at Bel Haven College graduation. On the way back I called home, only to learn that Gigi had driven the whole crowd over the mountain in the jeep, demolishing it and injuring several passengers—none seriously. Needless to say, the rest of the flight home seemed endless.

I arrived to find Franklin with several stitches in his head, the guest with a badly bruised thigh, the jeep pretty well totaled, Bunny complaining that her arm hurt, and Gigi near tears at the mention of the mishap.

Gigi had permission to drive from the gate to the house, but I did not know that she was going to extend this from the house, up around the mountain to the distant Reid field, and back. It was on the way back that she hit a spongy spot in the road where water from a little spring crossed. The road gave way and down the jeep went, turning over several times. We were only grateful that it was not more serious.

Bunny continued to complain about her arm, but since it was neither discolored nor swollen, we told her to forget it. But the complaining continued for several weeks. Finally, to settle the matter, I took her to an orthopedic surgeon. An X-ray showed a fractured arm. From then on, whenever Bunny complained, we listened.

Fret not thyself, it tendeth only to evil.

—Psalm 37:8 rsv

How many mistakes I have made with the children because I was fretting, concerned to the point of worry. Invariably it prompted me to unwise action. Sharpness, unfair punishment, too severe discipline—even my attitude and tone of voice. But a mother who walks with God knows He only asks her to take care of the possible and to trust Him for the impossible.

The Other Cheek

~

On hearing indignant wails from the kitchen, I looked in to see what was happening. Bunny, age three, was holding her hand to her cheek and eying Anne reproachfully.

"What on earth's the matter?" I demanded.

"Mommy," replied five-year-old Anne patiently, "I'm teaching Bunny about the Bible. I'm slapping her on one cheek and teaching her to turn the other one so I can slap it, too."

"One, Two, Free"

～

Franklin, at age three, managed to get into everybody's hair. I never knew one small boy could be so omnipresent. He was lovable and stubborn, reserved, surprisingly tender at times, and an incorrigible tease. I have seen all three sisters in tears and Franklin still laughing gleefully.

He went through a spitting stage. I don't know where he picked up that one.

Johnny and Tommy Frist were teenagers then, summering in Montreat. They enjoyed Franklin, and when the rest of us would be ready to send him to the pound, they would still be laughing good-naturedly.

One day, Johnny was up here bantering with Franklin, who

had gone through his whole repertoire—spitting and all. Johnny had warned, "You spit one more time and you'll be sorry!"

Franklin spit. So Johnny picked him up and, still chuckling, stuffed him in the woodbin built into the stone wall by the kitchen fireplace, and latched the door.

All was quiet. We looked at one another. Johnny, still grinning, pushed his blond hair back off his forehead and waited.

Soon a small voice said, "Okay. I'll count ten for you t' let me out'n here."

Quiet.

"One. Two. Free. . ."

Quiet again.

"One. Two. Free. . ."

Again, silence.

Finally, Johnny broke the silence. "What's the matter in there, Franklin? Why'd you stop?"

"Can't count any higher," he replied, in a somewhat subdued voice.

The Offering

~

Music played quietly as the offering plate reached our row. Out of the corner of my eye, I saw Franklin dip his hand into the offering.

Quick as a flash, I grabbed the five-year-old fist.

Looking up, an aggrieved expression on his little-boy face, he exclaimed loud enough for all about us to hear, "I was only hiding my penny under his dollar."

Aware of the suppressed smiles around us, I could only think of how often I had been guilty of the same thing: trying to hide my penny under someone else's dollar.

Meanwhile, the people in Judah said, "The strength of the laborers is giving out, and there is so much rubble that we cannot rebuild the wall."

—NEHEMIAH 4:10

How often I have felt that way!

The Thought That Counts

~

Ned arrived after we moved up on the mountain. There is a picture of us in the big old brass bed in our room, with Bill and the four older ones watching him with pride and appreciation.

I can still see Franklin, five years old by then, never one to dress up much if he could help it. He clomped as quietly as his cowboy boots let him, guns and holsters slung low around the hips that were barely there, a big glass of milk clutched in both grimy hands, sloshing precariously.

"So you'll have plenty of milk," he explained.

I refrained from explaining that a cow does not drink milk to make milk. It was the thought that counted.

He's Not a Load

~~~

Nearly three years later, looking out of the upstairs corner window, I saw a picture that impressed itself indelibly on my memory. Franklin was now nearly eight, and Ned, around three.

Abandoning the curvy driveway, they were taking a shortcut straight up the side of the mountain. The steepness was too much for little Ned, who slipped and started to fall. As always, quick on the draw, Franklin caught him, then kneeling down, helped Ned scramble up on his back. Grasping him firmly under the knees, Franklin struggled up the mountain with his added load.

In the intervening years when, because of the difference in age and temperaments, they were not so close, that picture kept coming to mind and I knew that eventually, that was the way it would be. Not necessarily the older supporting the younger, but each one helping the other.

Bicycle Prayers

~

$\mathcal{N}$ ed had reached the point in life when he wanted a bicycle more than anything. He had been playing with Joel Barker that fall, and he wanted one just like Joel's.

"Today!"

"No," Bill said. "Wait until Christmas."

And that was that.

So Joel lent Ned his new bike for a week. Before the week was over, Ned knew that Joel's bike would be too small for him in a few months. So he decided he needed a larger, ten-speed model.

The next week he saw one advertised in Sears with three

speeds, stick shift, spring suspension, butterfly handles, triple brakes, slicks—the works!

This was the one he *had* to have (and it was still two months until Christmas)!

Then I understood, as never before, why God does not answer all of our prayers right away. Today we may be beseeching Him for things we would not want six months from now.

However, most of our prayers are not "bicycle prayers." When we pray according to God's will (that the prodigal may return; that the sorrowing may find His comfort; that He will work each situation out for our good and His glory), He hears us. For we know that each of these requests is what He wants.

But at times He has us wait for the answers.

The command "Wait on the Lord," found in Psalm 27:14, reads in the old Prayer Book Version (which is older than our King James Version): "O tarry thou in the Lord's leisure."

And to many of us impatient souls, how "leisurely" He seems at times!

Still Time

~

*D*ear Journal,

With Franklin, I did not intend to push him to put his trust in Christ. But my heart would have rested easier if I knew that those small, rough hands were in His. If I knew there was a concern—a conviction of sin. In fact, I wonder if he was really aware of it, even.

Once I had a dream and Franklin was a young man, attractive, brushing aside all concern for his spiritual welfare. Unreachable. I awoke with a dread and a sickness, only to find it was a dream. He was still a little boy at home with us.

There was still time.

Love which outlives
All sin and wrong, Compassion which forgives
To the uttermost, and justice whose clear eyes
Through lapse and failure look to the intent
And judge our frailty by the things we meant.

—J. G. WHITTIER

He who fears the LORD has a secure fortress,
and for his children it will be a refuge.

—PROVERBS 14:26

The Bible Says

~

Franklin was polishing his shoes on the hearth. Beatrice Long, who helped us for more than thirty years, overheard him ask Ned, "Ned, do you love me?"

Ned answered thoughtfully, "Yes, Nock. I love you."

"Well," came the heartless reply, "I don't love you."

Ned leaned back against the stone hearth and thought a minute. "Well, I love you."

"Well, I don't love you."

"The Bible says—"

Franklin cut him off. "The Bible doesn't say I have to love you, does it?"

"Well . . . the Bible says some nice things."

David's prayer for Solomon: "Long may he live! May gold from Sheba be given him. May people ever pray for him and bless him all day long."

—PSALM 72:15

Wouldn't it be wonderful if mothers and fathers took this suggestion to heart: to pray continually and praise daily?

He's Okay

~

Franklin had Ned trained to stand outside his door rather than entering. One night as I was tucking Franklin in, a small, pajamaed figure appeared at the door.

"Nock, can I come in and kiss you good night?" Permission granted, he did and trotted off to bed.

"You know," Franklin confided to me, "he's a pretty good little boy."

Hard Work

~

How often our children reflect our attitudes. Ned was three and a half years old. "My playing school," he announced.

"Is it fun?" I asked unnecessarily, as he was obviously enjoying himself.

"No," he replied with a sigh, "it's hard work!"

Sunshine

〰️

Tucking Ned in bed one night, I leaned down to kiss him good night.

Looking closely at my face, a delighted smile spread over his. "It looks just like sunshine," he said.

"What looks like sunshine?" I asked.

And his fingers gently touched the lines going out from the corners of my eyes.

With such an observation, how could anyone mind growing old?

Rough Times

~

There were times in kindergarten when things got rough for Ned.

"There's one boy at school what'n I don't like."

"Why?"

"Him always picks on me."

"How?"

"Every time my knock his blocks down," Ned explained indignantly, "him tells the teacher on me."

Unless the LORD builds the house, its builders labor in vain.
Unless the LORD watches over the city, the watchmen
    stand guard in vain.
In vain you rise early and stay up late,
toiling for food to eat—for he grants sleep to those he loves.
Sons are a heritage from the LORD, children a reward
    from him.
Like arrows in the hands of a warrior are sons
    born in one's youth.
Blessed is the man whose quiver is full of them.
They will not be put to shame when they contend with
    their enemies in the gate.

—PSALM 127

Martha Luther King

~~~

"Mom, you know when Martha Luther King was here this summer?" Ned asked.

"Yes."

"Well, some of the children in the clubs, you know? Some of them said to me, 'Martha Luther King is gooder'n your daddy.' And I said, 'Aw, shut up!'"

"That wasn't very nice," I remonstrated. "They have a right to their own opinions."

"Then," he continued, ignoring my reaction, "you know what I think happened?"

"What?"

"I think I hit one of them."

"Ned!" I exclaimed sharply. "That really wasn't nice."

Ned's eyes danced gleefully. "And you know what?"

"What?"

"I enjoyed it, too!"

Encouragement

~

An anxious heart weighs a man down, but a kind word cheers him up.

—PROVERBS 12:25

Dear Journal,

Never let a single day pass without saying an encouraging word to each child.

Particularly wherever you have noticed any—even the slightest—improvement on some weak point. Some point at which you have been picking and criticizing.

And never fail to pass on any nice thing you have heard said about anyone to that child.

In David's prayer for Solomon, he said, ". . . prayer also shall be made for him continually; and daily shall he be praised" (Ps. 72:15 KJV).

"More people fail for lack of encouragement," someone wrote, "than for any other reason."

Storms

~

The rumble of thunder was only a distant threat. But the wind in the firs beside the stream, and the oaks and the pines between the bedroom window and the street, announced the storm was on its way.

All my life I have loved storms. But then, I have only experienced them from the shelter of a solidly built house, and as a child, with the warm conviction that with Mother and Daddy near, nothing really bad could happen.

The wind rose menacingly, and there was a sudden crack of thunder directly overhead. Soon I heard the patter of little feet and sensed a small presence in the room. I heard a whispered "Mother?" That was all.

The covers were thrown back in comforting welcome as one or more small, night-clad forms slipped in (depending on the severity of the storm). There, lovingly encircled, we snuggled safely together under the covers, listening to the storm, unafraid. As nature once more grew quiet, we drifted off to sleep.

It was later, when I knew they were all enduring their own individual storms, that I lay awake wishing I could share them.

At night, it was as if I could hear a whispered "Mother?" Only there was no one there. I sensed the distant thunder, and all I could do was pray.

One Got Lost

~

"Look, Mom!" Franklin called excitedly. "Look! The clouds broke to pieces and one got lost!"

I looked out across the valley and, sure enough, the passing storm was dissipating and a little cloud had gotten lost in one of the coves.

Little did we know that the time would come years later when we were the clouds and Franklin got lost.

There were calls from school principals, headmasters, irate teachers, even the police. The last called indignantly one night to say that Franklin had slammed the gate to our property in his face.

I urged the policeman to come up for a talk, assuring him that the gate would be open and I would have a pot of coffee ready. Franklin was, as usual, totally unrepentant and grinning like a possum. Apparently he had passed the local policeman, who had either caught him speeding or thought (from force of habit) he was speeding, and the policeman took off after him. Whereupon Franklin stepped on the gas and made it to the property in time to slam the electric gate and walk in the house chuckling.

I'm not sure teenagers always appreciate the value of the police.

Years ago during college, when we summered with Grandmother Bell in the Shenandoah Valley of Virginia, my sister Rosa and I taught daily Vacation Bible School up in the mountains. I was teaching my little group the Beatitudes and one day called on one of them to recite. The only mistake I remembered was, "Blessed are the policemakers," and I'm not sure it was a mistake.

Anyway, the policeman showed up shortly. We sat around the kitchen fire drinking coffee and discussing various subjects, finally getting around to the situation. To this day I don't know whether Franklin was speeding or not. I'm not even convinced the policeman was convinced. But we did apologize for the gate slammed in his face, which Franklin considered fun, I considered rude, and the policeman considered infuriating. And that particular episode came to a friendly conclusion.

But there were other episodes, other complaints, other phone calls.

If God will graciously satisfy each child early with His unfailing love, that they may rejoice and be glad in Him all their days (Psalm 90:14), this will be enough.

Worry and Worship

～

There is no situation so chaotic that God cannot from that situation, create something that is surpassingly good. He did it at the creation. He did it at the cross. He is doing it today.

—BISHOP MOULE

It was early in the morning in another country. Exhausted as I was, I awoke around three o'clock. The name of someone I loved dearly flashed into my mind. It was like an electric shock. Instantly I was wide-awake. I knew there would be no more sleep for me the rest of the night. So I lay there and prayed for the one who was trying hard to run away from God. When it is dark and the imagination runs wild, there are fears that only a mother can understand.

Suddenly the Lord said to me, *Quit studying the problems and start studying the promises.* Now God has never spoken to me audibly, but there is no mistaking when He speaks.

So I turned on the light, got out my Bible, and the first verse that came to me was Philippians 4:6–7: "Be careful for nothing; but in every thing by prayer and supplication with thanksgiving let your requests be made known unto God. And the peace of God, which passeth all understanding, shall keep your hearts and minds through Christ Jesus" (KJV). Or, as the Amplified Version has it, "Do not fret or have any anxiety about anything, but in every circumstance and in everything by prayer and petition [definite requests] *with thanksgiving* continue to make your wants known to God" (my italics).

Suddenly I realized the missing ingredient in my prayers

had been "with thanksgiving." So I put down my Bible and spent time worshiping Him for who He is and what He is. This covers more territory than any one mortal can comprehend. Even contemplating what little we do know dissolves doubts, reinforces faith, and restores joy. I began to thank God for giving me this one I loved so dearly in the first place. I even thanked Him for the difficult spots that taught me so much.

And you know what happened? It was as if suddenly someone turned on the lights in my mind and heart, and the little fears and worries which, like mice and cockroaches, had been nibbling away in the darkness, suddenly scuttled for cover.

That was when I learned that worship and worry cannot live in the same heart: They are mutually exclusive.

The Hound of Heaven

~

We were just beginning family prayers one morning, gathered around the fireplace in the kitchen, when Mr. Sawyer, our contractor, came in. (We had moved into this house before it was quite finished.)

Now Mr. Sawyer was an old family friend. He had remodeled Mother and Daddy's home for them; he had remodeled our first little house in the valley; he had remodeled the little cabin on the mountain before we built this house. He had undertaken to do this one, which was somewhat more complicated, being built largely from scratch out of old log cabins and material salvaged from old houses.

But I am getting sidetracked. This is not about salvaging old materials but salvaging a boy.

Mr. Sawyer, clad in his crumpled khaki pants and plaid shirt, poked his unshaven face in the kitchen door. We explained that we were just beginning family prayers and asked him to join us. That day I had passed around small cards, on each of which was printed a Scripture verse. We would go around the room, each child and adult taking a turn reading the verse on his or her card.

Now Mr. Sawyer had the interesting habit of cleaning his glasses between his thumb and his forefinger. At times, noticing the cloudy condition of the glasses, I marveled that he was able to see through them. His verse that morning was, "Whom the Lord loveth He chasteneth" (Heb. 12:6 KJV).

But the way Mr. Sawyer read it, it came out, "Whom the Lord loveth, He chaseth."

It was just what I needed.

For Franklin, the "Hound of Heaven" was closing in.

How long ago was that? Yesterday? Twenty-five years ago?

Franklin just called to check on me. When Bill is away, he calls from time to time to make sure I am all right. I appreciate it.

Franklin has a terrific little wife now and his own three sons, "as good as they can be, and as bad as they can get away with," just like he was. He deserves each one. And may they give him as much fun (and frustration) as he gave me—and as much joy when they are grown.

Little Black Lamb

⌇

I was reading Psalm 139:7–12, putting a certain loved name in appropriately. Suddenly I realized this was another side of Luke 15, the parable of the lost sheep.

With such a Shepherd, that lost sheep hadn't a chance.

When Franklin was born, Luverne Gustavson, Bill's secretary at that time, gave him a little stuffed black lamb containing a music box that, when wound, played "Jesus Loves Me." It is on the bookshelf in my bedroom now beside a picture of Franklin in Israel holding a little black lamb.

Prophetic? Almost.

A comfort? Frequently.

Fleeing from you
nothing he sees
of your going before him
as he flees.
Choosing his own paths
how could he know
your hand directs where
he shall go?
Thinking himself free
—free at last—
unaware your right hand
holds him fast.

The Prodigal's Parents

~~

Much has been written and said about the prodigal son. What about the parents?

I have seen them at times—bravely facing other parents who, like them, had done everything right, and whose children had chosen to follow Christ, while theirs had rejected the Truth and gone.

How, I wondered, did Monica, the mother of Augustine, feel among her friends during those years when her brilliant young son, a leader of the heretical "Manichees," lived in open defiance of God and the Church? (See *Augustine*, by Louis Bertrand.)

How did Jim Vaus's parents feel? His father was an ordained Baptist minister, yet his son was repeatedly caught cheating or stealing, all the while charading as a Christian. After a stint in the navy, he received a dishonorable discharge and eventually wound up seriously involved with the underworld network of crime.

They felt good eyes upon them
and shrank within—undone;
good parents had good children
and they a wandering one.
The good folk never meant
to act smug or condemn,
but having prodigals
just "wasn't done" with them.
Remind them gently, Lord,
how You
have trouble with Your children,
too.

Failures

~

*C*olleen Evans, in her challenging book *Start Loving*, quotes a friend who had written her:

Our failures. That's the hardest area, especially when they have affected the lives of our loved ones. As our two children step out into the adult world it is a joy to see many beautiful things in their lives. But it hurts to see areas of need and struggle that stem in part from ways we have failed them.

A friend reminded me recently that even these areas are part of the "all things" which God will use to make a man and a woman who will accomplish His unique purposes.

So when thoughts of my failures push their way into my consciousness, I let His total forgiveness dissolve my regrets, and go on to praise Him who accepts us just as we are and lovingly works to make us more than we are.

He doesn't expect us—or our children—to be finished products now.

Spiritual Drought

~

Bill was away in Rio de Janeiro addressing the Baptist World Alliance that summer.

My job was to pack five little Grahams and myself for a summer to be spent in Switzerland. (I offered to go and address the Baptists while he packed and prepared the five little Grahams for Switzerland, but the idea was not received with enthusiasm.)

Only a mother who has tried to pack for herself plus five children for several months in a foreign country will know the difficulty of the job.

Finally, preparations were finished and we departed for

Switzerland. After a long and tiring day, the plane landed in Geneva. We were met by the Tchividjians, our hosts for the summer.

I was too tired that night to notice much. I just felt the warmth of their welcome and the coolness of the linen sheets after everyone had departed and the children had been safely tucked in bed.

The next morning when I woke and pulled up the rolling blinds, I found myself looking out over Lake Geneva and the snow-capped mountains beyond rising to the majestic Dents du Midi. Everything was utterly charming and peaceful.

That is, until the children woke. Keeping house in Europe, I found, is considerably different from keeping house in America. Grocery shopping needed to be done every day. Not only that, instead of supermarkets there were small shops for each particular item: the butcher shop, cheese shop, grocery, fruit stand, and so forth. Our bread was delivered daily to us freshly baked, unwrapped, sticking out of the basket on the back of the bread boy's bicycle. Long, skinny French loaves, crusty on the outside, light and scarce on the inside.

So I found a good part of my time taken up simply in keeping the family fed and the house run. The result? Spiritual drought.

For me, spiritual dryness usually follows an extremely busy period. Air must be still for dew to fall, and I was anything but still.

One day, Bob and Myrl Glockner, who were spending the summer in a nearby hotel, came by; collected our five children and Gigi's high-school roommate, Dorothy Mayell, who was our houseguest; and took them off for the day.

I grabbed my Bible, found an empty chaise on the portico leading from the dining room to the front yard, and there, in the sun, I read Job all day.

I felt like the prophet, fed by angels in the desert when he had reached the end of himself—fed and refreshed. And, we are told, he went in the strength of that food forty days and forty nights.

When the car pulled up the drive and through the iron gates late that afternoon, all the occupants piled out, tired but happy, full of the day's experiences. Supper was waiting, and their mother was refreshed and eager to have them back.

> Drifting . . . slipping . . . slow I went;
> no leap in sudden haste,
> but quietly I eased away
> into this silent waste.
> How long it's been, I do not know;
> a minute from Him seems
> like long midnights of emptiness
> and silent screams.
> I heard the distant promises
> with wistfulness; and groped to see
> a glimmer of Him in the dark:
> Could He see me?
> There was no pounding on the Gates,

—no cry at Heaven's door . . .
I had no strength; my tears left
a puddle on the floor.
Then from my crumpled nothingness,
my dungeon of despair,
a quiet opening of the door
—a breath of Living air.
He let me sleep, as if I'd died,
yet when the morning broke
the Risen Son discovered me,
and I awoke.
New, I awoke; His warming love,
updrawing, transformed everything.
Tell me—is this how an acorn feels
in Spring?

Prayer of a
Middle-Aged Woman

~

Dear Lord,
Thou knowest better than I myself that I am growing older and will someday be old. Keep me from the fatal habit of thinking I must say something on every subject and on every occasion. Release me from craving to straighten out everybody's affairs. Make me thoughtful but not moody, helpful but not bossy. With my vast store of wisdom, it seems a pity not to use it all, but Thou knowest, Lord, that I must have a few friends at the end.

Keep my mind free from the recital of endless details; give me wings to get to the point. Seal my lips on my aches and pains. They are increasing, and love of rehearsing them is becoming sweeter as the years go by. I dare not ask for grace enough to enjoy the tales of others' pains, but help me to endure them with patience.

Give me a growing humility and a lessening cocksureness when my memory seems to clash with the memories of others. Teach me the glorious lesson that occasionally I may be mistaken. Keep me reasonably sweet . . . and not hard to live with . . . for a sour old person is one of the crowning works of the devil. Give me the ability to see good things in unexpected places, and talents in unexpected people. And give me the grace to tell them so.

It Isn't Easy Growing Up in Today's World

~

It isn't easy growing up in today's world. Pressures to conform—to be "in"—to be "with it." Pressures to rebel. A materialistic, secular society and the false standard created by it. There are no moral absolutes left in the world. Instead of "Thou shalt not," it is "Why not?"

Our children are facing pressures, temptations, and problems we never had to face before.

A few years back the two-lane highway between the little town near which we live and the neighboring city was being widened to a four-lane highway. For several weeks after the blacktop had been laid there were no white lines to guide the traffic. If you want a frightening, confusing experience, try to drive down a four-lane highway with no white lines. During this period there was a head-on collision, and five people were killed.

Yet we turn our children loose today on the freeways of life with:

> no road signs
> no traffic rules
> no guardrails
> no center line
> no speed limit
> no stop signs
> in high-powered cars with faulty brakes.

And we wonder why they wreck!

Some years ago in Edinburgh I heard the Duchess of Hamilton say to a group of women, "It is important not only that we teach our children how to behave, we must teach them what to believe."

What must we teach them to believe? We must teach them as soon as they are old enough to talk that God loves them. We are to teach our children that the Lord Jesus died to save them from their badness.

Jesus put a little child in the midst of his disciples. He did not tell that child to become like his disciples; He told his disciples to become like that little child.

Never underestimate simple childlike faith.

An actress in London once asked me, "How do you explain the crucifixion to your children?"

Just as the Bible does—God dying for my sins.

Whatever you do, don't try to soften the horror or the glory of it. Explain it simply. Children know you love them—but not their dirt!

For instance, when they come into the house after they have been playing on a rainy day, they are required to wipe their feet, and if necessary, change their clothes and bathe. They know that you love them, *but not their dirt.*

And different stains require different treatment. There is a stain on the souls of men that nothing can remove but the life-blood of One completely holy and without sin.

Only God could qualify. (Had there been any other way, don't you think He would have taken it?) So God became man and died for us. Read them the great Bible stories, explaining to them the truths found there and help them to memorize its tremendous passages.

Teach them to fear the Lord in the finest, noblest sense of that grand old word, which is not merely to be scared of, but also is reverential trust. We are told, "in the fear of the Lord is strong confidence: and his children shall have a place of refuge."

And again, "the fear of the Lord is the beginning of wisdom."

The right sort of fear produces honor and obedience. We read in the Bible, "O that there were such an heart in them, that they would fear me, and keep all my commandments always, that it might be well with them and with their children forever!" (Deut. 5:29 KJV).

It is the fear of the Lord that puts all other fears in proper perspective.

Grandparents Are Special

~~

Although we were deprived of our natural grandparents while growing up in China, the senior missionaries were like our own grandparents—Uncle Jimmie and Aunt Sophie Graham, Dr. and Mrs. Woods, Grandma and Grandpa Reynolds, and others.

In the Orient, age was respected because it implied the accumulation of wisdom that the years bring. To have a grandparent in the home was considered a privilege rather than a burden.

Once when Bill and I were in Tokyo on our way to the Korean crusade, we were taking a walk in the Imperial Gardens, which were open for the enjoyment of the public.

It was a hot Sunday afternoon, and a strong wind blew grit in our faces. Lots of families were out.

As we descended a steep incline from the upper garden, we heard a gale of merry laughter. Turning the corner, we met a whole family—the smiling grandmother in her wheelchair being pushed by her son (I assume), who was bent double with the effort, and behind the son the daughter-in-law (?), in turn pushing the son, surrounded by the rest of the family, all hugely enjoying the ridiculousness and fun of it. I wished for my mother so that we could push her around those lovely gardens in her wheelchair.

Our children did not get to see as much of Bill's parents as we would have liked. They lived in Charlotte. But the children were deeply influenced by their paternal grandparents because of their kindly and godly lives. Fortunately we lived much closer to my parents. Living across the road from them was one of the nicest things that ever happened to our first four children. (Ned was born after the move up the mountain.)

They were ideal grandparents—strict disciplinarians but full of love and fun.

Many nights the girls would spend with their grandparents. I can still see them, like three little stairsteps, dressed for bed and hugging their favorite blankets or pillows, as they climbed our curving drive and walked the short distance across the road to Daddy and Mother's.

Those evenings were always family times, as they had been in China. Games to be played, books to be read aloud. Mother made clothes for their dolls, nursed them when they were sick, let them help her work in her flowers in the spring and rake leaves in the fall and lick the pan after making a batch of fudge.

Since Daddy was a doctor, whenever medication or stitches were needed, he was available.

Both were great storytellers. They were happy Christians. They were part of God's special provision for us during the many occasions Bill was away on crusades. Just as Jesus promised, "He who leaves family for My sake and the Gospel's shall receive an hundredfold in this life" (see Mark 10:29, 30).

Those of you who have not had a loving Christian heritage can make sure your children have one. Even if you feel it is too late, commit the wasted years and lost opportunities to God. Love each one who comes to mind, and pray.

Then, look around for some young person you can encourage and help along the way.

Empty Nests

~

It comes sooner or later to us all. All, that is, who have nests.

You have never seen a bird hanging onto her babies' tail feathers, with her beak herding them back into the nest when they would fly away. Quite the opposite: If the fledgling is reluctant, he is gently nudged out.

I had left Ned at a boarding school in England. The other children by now were either married or away in college. Bill was off on a crusade.

I dreaded returning to that now-empty house.

But as I entered the front door and looked down the length

of the hall and up the steps leading to the children's now-vacant rooms, suddenly it wasn't empty. I was greeted by a living Presence, and I realized anew how true His last words were: "Lo, I am with you" (Matt. 28:20 KJV). I was surrounded by loved memories and the comfortableness of knowing I was home. This was my base of operations.

Now the years ahead stretched vacant. What did God want me to do? Travel with Bill? I tried it for two years: two trips around the world—Manila, Hungary, Singapore, Poland, China, Europe. And I wound up a zombie. I cannot keep up with the man. In fact, taking me on a crusade is rather like a general taking his wife to battle with him. Our happiest times together are at home or on vacation (though he usually takes his vacations like the drivers of the Indianapolis 500 take their pit stops—as seldom and as quickly as possible).

So home is where I hope to stay for the most part. I hope to be here when any of the children or grandchildren need me. From my vantage point, I can look back on circumstances involving our children, situations I once felt were hopeless, only to see in disbelief and amazement as God brought order out of chaos, light out of darkness.

I will follow their struggles with peace in my heart. Battles may be lost, but God will win out in the end. We gave them to Him, each one uniquely loved, each as dear as the other: our most treasured possessions.

As each little family builds its nest, I shall be watching with interest and love, concern at times, but concern undergirded with confidence, knowing God is in control.

And I shall be enjoying life!